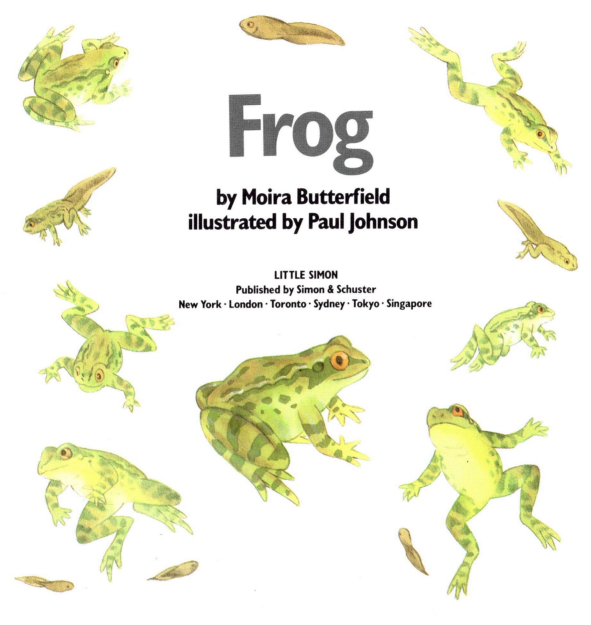

Frog

by Moira Butterfield
illustrated by Paul Johnson

LITTLE SIMON
Published by Simon & Schuster
New York · London · Toronto · Sydney · Tokyo · Singapore

A female frog lays a clump of eggs in a pond. They are called *frog-spawn*.

Each little black egg
is inside a round bag
of jelly that keeps
it safe.

After about a week
the egg grows a head
and a tail.

Soon the egg
becomes a tiny
tadpole. It wriggles
out of the bag
of jelly.

The tadpole eats very small plants that float in the water.

It wriggles its tail to swim along.

It can breathe underwater through gills. They look like feathery fingers.

After five weeks
the tadpole grows
back legs.

The feathery gills disappear.

The tadpole grows lungs.

Now it must breathe air like we do.

It comes up for air
every now and again.

Soon the tadpole grows front legs. Its tail starts to shrink.

After fifteen weeks it is a tiny frog. It leaves the pond to live on land.

It has strong back legs for jumping.

It catches beetles, insects, and worms to eat.

The frog grows bigger and bigger.

After about three years it is ready to make its own frog-spawn.